C

D0348067

First Published 2018
Copyright©2018 by Deedee Cuddihy

No part of this book may be
reproduced, except for short extracts
for quotation or review, without the
written permission of the publisher
(unless it's the bits that I borrowed
myself, of course . . .)

ISBN 978 0 9930986 4 2

Published by Deedee Cuddihy
10 Otago Street,
Glasgow G12 8JH
Scotland

Cover design, graphics assistance and
research: Anonymous (Glasgow) Ltd.

Printed and bound in Great Britain by
Bell and Bain Ltd, Glasgow

Dedication

This book is dedicated, with the kind permission of her family, to the late, great *Hazel Duff* whose Facebook post about porridge sparked it all off.

And particular thanks, also, to members of Merchant Voices Community Choir and the International Club at Wellington Church for their many contributions.

Foreword

Like a good number of the people who contributed to this book, I was a child who hated porridge (or "oatmeal" as we called it in America where I grew up). My older brother, Bob, liked it but I was the one who scraped it into the bushes outside the dining room window and then told my mother I had eaten it all up! Fast forward to my early teenage years and my arrival at a small, independent boarding school in Dumfries and Galloway where, to earn extra pocket money, you could sign up to make the breakfast. I quickly got the hang of making porridge on the kitchen Aga although I never got used to getting my whisk-wielding hand burnt when an occasional spray of lava-hot cereal erupted from the pot. And I learned to love porridge, served with creamy milk and brown sugar which is how most of us ate it at the school in the early 1960s. It is amazing to see how popular porridge has become throughout the UK in recent years, something which would surely have Dr. Samuel Johnson - the man who famously declared that "in England we wouldn't think of eating oats" - birling in his Westminster Abbey grave.

"Porridge is so familiar to so many people. Everyone has a story about porridge."

(Alex Hely-Hutchinson, owner of the 26 Grains porridge cafe in London, interviewed on BBC Radio)

The last time I had porridge was in the jail. I used to have Ready Brek when I was a kid. We did have porridge sometimes and it was porridge with salt but Ready Brek with sugar. They give you sachets of porridge at the soup kitchen too, if you want it.

(Ed)

The food that's never let me down in life is porridge, especially with milk and maple syrup, which is delicious.

(singer Marianne Faithfull interviewed in The Guardian)

I love porridge. I soak the oatmeal overnight then let it cook while I'm doing Pilates. I eat it with maple syrup.

(Anne)

I've always hated porridge and I never eat it. Having said that, I spent one of my first student placements, in the late 1960s, at Perth Royal Infirmary where I worked the night shift in the kitchen, cooking breakfast for 450 patients, entirely on my own. The porridge was made in a free-standing, steam jacketed boiler which came up to my waist. You'd pour in gallons of water and pounds of oats and then stir it with a giant wooden paddle, cooking it for hours until it was eventually served up to the patients at about 7 in the morning.

(Maggie)

"Great-granddad may be forced to have porridge for Christmas dinner after Airdrie hospital lost his false teeth."

(news headline, 2017)

My gran lived near us and I used to have porridge at her house. Aye, it was nice. She cooked it with salt and I had sugar on mine. My mum tried to make it but it wasn't as good as my gran's. It was either too lumpy or too watery. Everything was better at my gran's – not just the porridge.

(Michelle)

We didn't have porridge at home but when my brother and I went to spend weekends with our great aunts Cissie and Tina in Dumbarton, we had it there. I loved it. I had mine with top of the milk, or sometimes a bit of cream, with salt sprinkled on the top. Another treat at their house was toasted pancakes.

(Judith)

I'm from Ayrshire originally but I was brought up by my grandparents - granny Margaret and papa Bob - in Knightswood from when I was about eight. My gran was an amazing woman, so she was - made sure I never left the house in the morning without a bowl of cereal or porridge. They both made it but I preferred hers. We had it with sugar and milk. In fact, they were my dad's grandparents - so they were really my great-grandparents. I probably have porridge once a week now, on average, with honey, and sometimes maple syrup as a treat.

(Billy)

When I lived with my aunt and uncle outside Dundee, we had porridge every morning for breakfast. I think my uncle took his "straight" - without sugar. But I certainly had sugar, until I discovered Golden Syrup which made it much more palatable. In fact, I thought I had invented Golden Syrup with porridge and was a bit indignant when I found out that other people ate it that way as well. When I turned 16, I was allowed to have cornflakes instead which was a relief.

(Caryl)

I'm the eldest of six children, from Blantyre, a Lanarkshire mining town, and we had porridge for breakfast, usually made by my mum but occasionally by my dad. He ate his with salt but we had sugar on ours. This was back in the 1940s and we got our milk from a farm up the road, brought around by Tam Weir with his pony and cart, in two big metal churns. The women would come out with milk jugs and get them filled up. Now I have my porridge with a few grains of that pink Himilayan salt sprinkled on top, and sometimes some plain yogurt with a little cinnamon. *If I can't get to sleep, I'll have some porridge at one in the morning and that does the trick.*

(Ann Marie)

My mother didn't know how to cook when she first got married but she eventually got the hang of porridge. We had it plain, with milk, but no sugar, although we'd occasionally sneak some honey on to it. If there was any porridge left over, my mum fried it up the next morning with bacon. *This was in the 1950s, in Maybole, when the milk was brought around by a man with a green cart, pulled by a skewbald horse. We had two milk cans, a pint and a two pint size and you'd bring one or both of them out to be filled up. There were no fridges, so the milk went into the pantry, with a plate on top, then you'd decant some into a jug and cover that with a muslin circle with beads sewn all around the edge to weigh it down.*

(Linda)

Fried Porridge

Shape cold porridge (preferrably chilled in the fridge) into thinnish cakes (having made the porridge with one part oats to no more than two parts water), pat both sides with flour, then fry gently in a little hot butter or bacon fat. Serve with Golden Syrup.

(adapted from a recipe for Fried Mush in the Fanny Farmer Cookbook)

We didn't have porridge in our house. It was Ready Brek – or Ready Boak, as one of my friends used to call it. I've never made porridge. I'm not really a breakfast person. I'm more a grab a cup of tea before work, then eat a packet of biscuits at 11am because I'm starving kind of person. I did buy a pot of that instant stuff, because I'm needing to lose weight, but I haven't actually eaten it yet. I thought it might do for lunch.

(Adam)

When I was 13, I went to boarding school and we got porridge for breakfast there. Aye, it was alright. It would keep you going all day which was just as well because most of the food was rotten so at least I could skip lunch. We had Ready Brek at home. There was an iconic advert for it, in the days when there were only three TV channels. It showed a boy with a glowing stomach.

(Gilmour)

"Porridge is disappearing from the breakfast menus of Britain's prisons, much to the disgust of inmates. Instead of the staple fare immortalised in the late Ronnie Barker's TV series, many prisoners are now served up a 27p breakfast pack containing cereal, bread, jam, tea or coffee and UHT milk."

(news report, 2006)

My mum made us porridge every morning in winter before we went to school. She'd put the bowls to cool on the windowsill while we were upstairs getting ready. It was lovely. We had it with sugar - caster sugar - and my mum used oatmeal, not porridge oats. There were five of us kids so it would be a cheap way to feed us. I really liked it. I think we all did. But that wouldn't have made any difference because that's all there was - and we weren't allowed to leave for school without eating it. *I make porridge for my own kids but its with sachets, in the microwave. It's delicious.*

(Ruth)

"Someone's been eating my porridge" growled Papa bear.

"Someone's been eating my porridge" said Mama bear.

"Someone's been eating my porridge and they ate it all up!" cried Baby bear.

(from "Goldilocks and the Three Bears")

There were five of us kids and my mum used to make us porridge but it was too thick for me and I'd say: "Can't you make it thinner - but not really thin?" All the rest of them had sugar with theirs but I had salt - just a bit sprinkled on top. Aye - I was always different from the others. I'm the only one who went into drugs.

(Tracey)

Since 1984, scientists at Harvard University's School of Public Health have been following the dietary habits of around 100,000 people and have now come to the conclusion that those of us who regularly eat whole grains, such as porridge oats, can expect to live longer and healthier lives. Just one small bowl of porridge a day can increase life expectancy by 5 per cent, and reduce the risk of death by heart disease by 9 per cent.

(The Scotsman)

Scotland's oldest woman, Miss Jessie Gallan who has just celebrated her 109th birthday, says that the secret to a long life is eating a bowl of porridge every morning - and staying away from men.

(news report, 2015)

My nana, my mum's mum, had porridge every day of her life and she was 94 when she died. Just with a bit of milk. My parents had it occasionally. I don't make it but we always have porridge oats in the cupboard and I use them for fruit crumble mix and flap jacks and I'll put some in yogurt with fruit.

(Shona)

We had porridge and I hated it. I hated everything about it. My mother would put it in front of me and I'd just play around with it, although my two brothers ate theirs. Eventually she gave up and let me have bread and butter for breakfast, or toast. I'm 96 and I've never had porridge since. Maybe that's why I've lived so long!

(May)

Samuel Johnson: *"In England we wouldn't think of eating oats. We only feed them to horses."*

James Boswell: *"Well, maybe that's why in England you have better horses, and in Scotland we have better men".*

(Conversation, circa 1790, in response to Johnson criticising Boswell for the latter's Scottish habit of eating oats for breakfast.)

As Alan Davidson points out in The Oxford Companion to Food, porridge is a descendant of pottage, a thoroughly English institution, and the fact that most of us buy porridge oats in a box bearing a picture of a kilted Scotsman should not trick us into thinking that the Scots invented it.

(Elizabeth Grice)

Being English, we didn't have porridge when I was growing up. The first time I encountered it, I was four and I was having my adenoids taken out. This was in the days before the NHS. I was in a nursing home in Cheshire and a nurse appeared with a bowl of what she told me was porridge and I took one look at it and said I couldn't eat it. Maybe I had tried a mouthful because I knew it had a terrible consistency which meant it slipped down your throat. I said: "You don't understand - I don't want it!" and that was the end of porridge for me. *I've never had it since, even though I've lived in Scotland for over 50 years now.*

(Lis)

I'm from Yorkshire and we didn't have a lot of money when I was growing up so I suppose we had porridge because it was cheap. It was just my mum and me at home. She cooked the oats in water with a bit of salt and we ate it with milk but no sugar. But when my mum went back to work, I got sent to a childminder who also made me porridge but she served it with sugar which was even nicer. *The next time my mum put porridge in front of me, I tried a few mouthfulls and then put my spoon down. She said: "What's wrong?" and I said the childminder puts sugar on and I really like it that way. Yeah, she was okay with that and let me have sugar from then on.*

(George)

My dad is from Missouri and I make porridge the way he did when we were kids. Boil up water with a bit of salt, cut up an apple and cook it in the water until it's a bit soft – but not mushy – add some raisins, then the oats; stir from time to time; cook until the oats have soaked up all the water, then add some butter and honey.

(Sophie)

We had oatmeal in our house in Minnesota where I'm from. I think American oatmeal is different from Scottish porridge. I had Quaker instant oatmeal in a special Quaker Oats bowl. It was pink and turned purple when you put the hot oatmeal into it. Or was it purple and turned pink? Over here, in Scotland, to replicate the oatmeal I had as a child, I buy the biggest porridge oats possible and mix them with powdered milk and put them with boiling water into the microwave. Then, to eat, I add some vanilla and white sugar, or vanilla sugar if I can get it, and a bit of milk and some raspberry coulis. *I'm married to a Finnish guy and they have porridge. It's terrible stuff. But they only have it at Christmas, so that's a blessing.*

(Lizy)

An Aberdeen doctor faced tough competition as he defended his World Porridge Making Champion title. But Dr Izhar Khan met his match when he was defeated at this year's event by Simon Rookyard, from Greater Manchester. Dr Khan won the title in 2014 using a special spurtle crafted by one of his patients. Now in its 22nd year and held at Carrbridge, near Aviemore, the hotly contested competition boasted a 20-strong international line up. The title of World Porridge Making Champion is awarded to the competitor who makes the best traditional porridge using only three ingredients – oatmeal, salt and water.

(Louise Aitken, Aberdeen Evening Express, 2015)

The first time I had porridge, I had come to Glasgow in 1962, as a student from Iraq, and the first morning I came into breakfast and a bowl of something was put in front of me and I said: "Is this cornflakes?" because that's what I thought everyone in the UK ate for breakfast and they said: "No, this is porridge." I remember I ate it with sugar. Many years later I came back to Glasgow and am now settled here with my family and usually I have bread and perhaps cheese for breakfast, but not cereal or porridge.

(Mahamad)

In Lithuania, we have porridge – made from a wheat grain, I think – but we usually have it for supper, with milk and jam and cinnamon, before going to bed.

(Mindie)

I eat porridge from time to time but we didn't have it much when I was a kid because my late mum was Lithuanian and I don't think breakfast porridge was a big part of their food culture. But then my sister-in-law got her hooked on the stuff - sweetened with honey! No one should have honey, or sugar, on their porridge.

(Scott)

No - I have never had porridge and I've been in Scotland for several years! Do they sell it in the supermarkets? I want to try it. In Syria, where I come from, we have bread and cheese for breakfast, and sometimes beans, and that's what I have here.

(Achmed)

In Iran, we have something like porridge. It's called haleem and it has turkey in it. But we use wheat for it, not oats. I like it. It's awesome. Yes, it's eaten for breakfast.

(Abtin)

Of course we had porridge in Russia! My mother made it for us and we ate it with milk and sugar. It was good.

(Svetlana)

We have something called Oat Soup in Syria where I'm from. You chop an onion and fry it in oil, then cut up some meat and cook it with the onion, then put some boiling water in that, then some oats, and boil it for five minutes, then season it with salt, black pepper and cinnamon and you can have it in the morning or at night. When I went away to university, I phoned my mother and asked her how to make it. *I can cook a lot of her dishes but my wife says: please don't cook, you make such a mess in the kitchen.*

(Nadar)

I've lived in Scotland for over 20 years and I still don't like porridge.

(Zada, from Bosnia)

There were four kids in our family and my parents weren't well off so it was porridge in our house for breakfast every morning when I was growing up in Clydebank. Just made with oats, water and salt, served with milk, no sugar. My mother made it. It was awful. I make it now and I'm much better at it than she was.

(Isobel)

The first thing I remember having for breakfast was toast but when I started secondary school, my mother went through a phase of giving us porridge. It was awful: thick and slimy at the same time. The porridge would be stuck to the bottom of the bowl and when you poured the milk in, it would lift off and float around - like islands in a lake. After about three or four days of this, I said to my mother: "I can't eat this " and we switched to cornflakes and other cereal. *But a Scots Porage Oats packet was always very prominent in the kitchen cabinet so I think my parents must have eaten it from time to time.*

(Charlie)

My mum used to make porridge for us and I hated it. It was lumpy and had a skin on it, although how she managed both of those things I don't know. I had Shreddies instead. I like porridge now that I make it myself, in the microwave in a pyrex jug, and then I add blueberries, mixed seeds and manuka honey. I started eating it because of the health benefits.

(Sheila)

I really like the lumps in porridge but i can never make them, does anyone know how. thanks if you do.

(from an internet forum)

We had porridge - me, my brother and sister - every morning, winter and summer. My mum usually made it, but sometimes my dad did, if he didn't have to go out to work. My mum was from the Highlands and used to make it with a huge amount of salt in the water; way too much. It was disgusting. We had to eat it - that's all there was. But if my mum wasn't looking, I'd feed mine to the dog. He loved it! My mother had quite a good sense of humour. We always made faces when we ate her porridge, it was so awful. And sometimes she'd say to us in the morning: "Guess what's for breakfast? Faces!"

(Jim)

Breakfast was a nightmare for me when I was a child because we had to eat porridge. It might not have been so bad if it had some texture to it, but the way my mother made it, it was very smooth. And when you poured the milk over it, it would lift off from the bottom of the bowl and float around. I think my father put jam on his. *As if porridge wasn't bad enough, my mother made us take a tablespoon of some awful stuff called Angiers emulsion as well as a red capsule of something called Adepalin. This was decades ago but the names are burned on my memory.*

(Moira)

49% of people in the UK eat porridge, according to market research firm Mintel, with 23% of people eating it daily. It says sales of hot cereals – largely made up of porridge – have almost doubled since 2008, hitting £241m in 2013, and volume sales rising by 25% to 81 million kg.

(from a news report, 2013)

My husband has porridge every morning, winter and summer, every day of the year, all year. He won't leave the house in the morning without it. He makes it in the microwave but always uses Scott's Porage Oats - it has to be Scott's - and not the sachets. He has it with milk but uses no salt or sugar. He also has an egg, boiled for exactly three and a quarter minutes.

(Dorothy)

We had porridge all the time when I was growing up. There were 11 of us - nine children and my mum and dad - so porridge was cheap, and nourishing. I was the eldest and I used to go to the grain shop for the porridge oats which were kept in big sacks on the floor, with a scoop in them, and you'd scoop however much you needed into a paper bag. We always got five scoops which might last a week. There were cats in the shop, to keep down the mice and rats, and there was one who hid behind the sacks and would scratch your arm when you put the scoop in.

(Maureen)

My dad was raised on oatmeal, and he could never get enough. I found some cooking on his stove when he passed away in his late 80s.

(from the internet)

My mum made us porridge. She steeped the oatmeal overnight. I refused to eat it because I hated the smell of it. My dad used to say: "You will eat it!" But I screamed and cried and eventually they accepted that I wouldn't so my mum gave me bread and milk saps instead - a slice of plain bread, Mother's Pride, broken up in a bowl and hot milk poured on top, with a bit of sugar. Lovely. *We never had breakfast cereal, not after the time my mum bought a box of Weetabix and the first biscuit she took out of the packet had a dead mouse in it.*

(Dorothy)

We had porridge for breakfast - milk, no sugar - for as long as I can remember and then one morning when I was seven I said to my mum: "I can't eat this." She grabbed me by the hair, pulled my head back and forced a spoonful of porridge into my mouth. As soon as it hit my stomach, it came right back up again. Then she realised I was serious so I got cornflakes after that. From that day on, I've never eaten porridge. I can't even sit at the same table as someone eating it. And my wife has it most mornings!

(Tom)

We were staying in a boarding house in Blackpool when I was 7 or 8 and at breakfast one morning, an older girl and her younger brother started having a terrible argument which ended with the girl grabbing her brother by the collar and pouring her porridge down his back. I remember him running out the door and shrieking as he thumped up the stairs to tell their parents. It put me off porridge for years.

(Isabel)

I often have porridge for breakfast. I toast the oats first and it really improves the flavour. You just toast them in the pot you're using. Put the oats in, stir them around for a few minutes; don't burn them, maybe just until they get a bit of colour, then pour in the water. I use boiling water rather than cold. I eat it with honey and full cream milk, preferrably. I used to have top of the milk but I don't think that exists anymore. I also like cheese for breakfast - and soup - and fish.

(Ann)

My mum's from Pakistan but she's lived here for years and she makes us porridge. She uses rolled oats and starts by melting just a little bit of butter in the pot and stirs the oats around in that until they brown a bit, then she pours in milk – 2 or 2 and a half cups to one cup of oats – and stirs it till it's done. Then we eat it with milk and sugar. It's delicious. Sometimes I'll have that after dinner, for a dessert.

(Saima)

Irn-Bru Porridge with a Tablet Topping

(two small helpings or one large one)

1 cup porridge oats (not the jumbo ones)
2 cups Irn-Bru (not the diet stuff)
Salt
Scottish Tablet (plain for preference)

Using a wooden spoon (preferrably), mix the oats, the Irn-Bru and a pinch of salt in a small saucepan. Bring to the boil, stirring all the while, then turn the heat down low and stir constantly until a good consistancy has been reached. Put the porridge into one or two bowls and shave the tablet on top (or cut the tablet into tiny cubes). Eat - without milk. Not advised for breakfast but makes a delicious and very sweet desert or snack.

I eat my porridge by taking a spoonfull of porridge and dipping it into Carnation Milk or cream - so you're eating hot with cold.

(Winnie)

We're from St. Andrew's and I remember my grandfather ate his porridge by dipping each spoonful of it into a cup of milk. He didn't have sugar on his but I did.

(Rebecca)

My father usually made the porridge. I had mine with milk and white sugar. I don't think brown was available then. There wasn't a choice of sugars after the war. But my father ate his - no sugar - by dipping every spoonful into a cup of milk. Now my son, who's 40, eats his the same way!

(Sheena)

Labour leader Jeremy Corbyn believes porridge will fuel him through the long journey to the 2022 election as he vows to defeat the Tories.

(from a news report, 2017)

It has been a staple dish in Scottish breakfast bowls for hundreds, if not thousands of years - although debate still rages if its best with sugar or not. And now porridge has been revealed as the dish of choice for business leaders as they fill up to start their days in high-powered boardrooms and offices across the UK.

(The Herald, 2016)

My mum always made porridge for us – no sugar. I didn't know people ate sugar with their porridge until I left home. The only time we didn't have porridge was when a cargo of American breakfast cereal came into the docks across the road from our house in Govan and the guys we knew who unloaded the ships would throw a box of it over the wall into our garden.

(Maureen)

We had porridge every morning when I was growing up - near the Scott's Porage Oats factory, as it happens, in Cupar. My mum made it. No sugar - no, we were "old school". Sometimes we had porridge twice a day because when we started school and my mum went back to work, we'd go to my gran's for lunch and might have it there as well.

(Geoff)

"We read by the gaslight,
we had nae T.V.,

Hot porridge for breakfast,
cold porridge for tea,"

(from "Farewell to Glasgow" by Jim
McLean)

I have porridge quite often. I use those Irish oats, in the microwave, no sugar. My dad always said: "Only sassenachs put sugar in porridge." He used to make porridge at the weekends and made quite a fuss about it. It was the only thing he knew how to make, apart from toast. He used a lot of salt, maybe too much. My wife is a purist and can't be doing with sachets and microwaves for her porridge. So we each make our own. But she does take sugar with hers so I tease her about that.

(Paul)

We always had porridge when I was growing up, here in Glasgow and up in Tiree when we went to visit my mum's parents. They had a croft and some goats so we sometimes had goat's milk with it. Aye, it was fine with goat's milk. We had it with salt, that was Scottish and having it with sugar, that was English. We didn't cook it with salt, you added salt afterwards. It brings out the taste of the oats.

(Tommy)

Visitors from abroad, especially the French, love having porridge for breakfast when they stay at the hotel. They love hearing about the right way to make it and the right way to eat it. We should have a piping in of the porridge ceremony! We serve it with a wee jug of double cream and some honey and we tell them to add a small amount of each to every spoonful of porridge. *My mum was brought up on the family farm in Aberdeenshire and they had porridge every morning. With sugar? Never! Ever! That would be sacrilige, as far as my mum was concerned.*

(Rosemary Brown, the Allan Ramsay Hotel)

Everyone in my family likes porridge. If you asked me what I wanted for breakfast, I'd always choose porridge . . . or a fry-up. My papa - that's my dad's father - has his with salt and my mum's mum has hers with sugar. I couldn't eat mine without sugar; two teaspoons of white, and a bit of milk. I wouldn't use a microwave to make my porridge. I do it the traditional way, in a pot, on the cooker.

(Darcae, 19)

Gordon's porridge-making
equipment.

The author's granddaughters eating
her porridge (and loving it!).

Spoiled for choice in the shops.

Fried Porridge

Save your breath to cool your porridge.

Porridge bowl

Irn-Bru porridge

We had porridge when we went on family camping trips, in the Ochil Hills. My grandfather came too, and we'd build a fire in the morning and when it had burned down to almost nothing, my mum would put a pot on and make the porridge. I never liked it. Even with sugar it was rank.

(Stewart)

I was brought up on a farm in Ayrshire and we always had porridge for breakfast. Nice and thick. No sugar - sugar with your porridge was an English thing. It wasn't rolled oats, it was proper oatmeal and it was kept in the scullery in a wooden chest with a sloping lid - I think it was called a garnel. It had two sections inside, one for oatmeal and one for flour. I remember it got put outside and used for storing the hens' feed when my mother had the kitchen modernised. We had cows so there were pans of milk in the dairy and you'd skim the cream off the top, and have that with your porridge.

(Morag)

When I got my ex battery hens, the lady advised me to give them warm porridge in the winter to keep out the cold. I did this last year with the addition of some dried fruit and honey. This is a wonderful insulator against the cold, but should I give it as an afternoon treat, or give it first thing in the morning as porridge is intended to be eaten? Any Scots chicken keepers out their?

(from the internet forum
<u>backyardchickens.com</u>)

I am not a Scot, well I am a little bit, but that's a whole 'nother story. Just wanted to say that when I want to give my chickens something like warm oatmeal, I give it to them late in the afternoons an hour or so before they go to roost. Gives them something warm and filling right before bed.

(from the internet forum backyardchickens.com)

We had porridge and I hated it. It's difficult to like something that has the consistancy of vomit. And we didn't have sugar. We were a strictly no-sugar family which was quite unusual in the 1960s. That's because my father was really into healthy eating. Even so, he would probably have thought that anyone who took sugar on their porridge was a big jessie.

(Cliff)

We had porridge, with white sugar. When I was growing up, almost everything we ate had sugar on it. If there was bacon or sausage fat in the frying pan, you'd take a piece of bread, wipe the pan with it, then sprinkle sugar on it. Delicious.

(Brian)

I take a lot of sugar in my porridge - brown sugar. I add it while I'm making it, and then I add even more "to taste" when I'm eating it.

(Joseph)

We had porridge for breakfast. That's just what you got. My father let me have sugar with it but my mother didn't. Sugar and tea were still on ration then and my dad used to swop his tea for sugar with one of the other guys in the steel works, so I could have it on my porridge.

(Blackie)

I'm Italian and I share a flat in Glasgow with other students. There's one guy from Luxembourg and another one from Sweden and they both have porridge every morning, with jam and cinnamon.

(Claudia)

My mother always drummed it into us that the only thing you needed with porridge was a bit of salt when you were cooking it and milk to eat it with. So when I was staying in a B&B near Inverness once, years ago, and saw a family of foreign tourists stirring jam and marmalade into their porridge at breakfast, I was shocked. I'd never seen anything like it. I had to stop myself from telling them: "No! You don't put jam or marmalade on porridge!"

(Les)

One of my regulars bought me a pot of that instant porridge from a coffee shop this morning. There was a wee container of jam with it and I said: "Jam? No way am I eating jam with porridge!"

(Tommy)

"But where porridge is concerned, tradition has some peculiar departures from the norm, not least in St Kilda where, for their morning porridge, a puffin was very often boiled in the oats."

(food writer, Sue Lawrence)

Chef Heston Blumenthal famously brought the humble porridge oat slithering bang up to date in 2003 with his snail porridge, a dish combining high-quality porridge oats with snails, butter, fennel and parma ham.

(James Brennan)

I hear the English love their morning porridge with a large spoonful of jellied eels mixed in.

(from the internet)

"My mother was always a lady, whether she was bargaining with the butcher, breaking in a skittish charwoman or stirring the porridge which I can see her doing, with the porridge stick in one hand and the other holding a copy of her favourite French literary magazine within two inches of her nose."

(portrait of the author's mother by Arthur Conan Doyle)

We had porridge. My mother made it in a big pot, stirring it with a spurtle. And if there was any left over, we'd have it the next day, cold, or sometimes fried.

(Vivienne)

I inherited my grandmother's spurtle. I don't know what type of wood it's made from but it doesn't appear to have worn down much despite all the use its had.

(Carol)

Depite having to eat porridge when I was a child, and hating it, I make porridge for myself now. I eat it with banana, a wee drop of milk and a bit of honey on the top. Scott's Porage Oats. As soon as I've made the porridge and put it in a bowl, I wash the pot up. It's a lot easier to get it clean if you wash it up immediately.

(Jim)

I make porridge for myself but not every morning. I live alone so I just eat it out of the pot – saves washing up a bowl.

(Joseph)

My mum made porridge for us but because I was the youngest, and spoiled rotten, I could have cornflakes instead if I wanted. But the main thing I remember about porridge was when the pot was put to steep in cold water in the kitchen sink, a skin would form around the inside of the pot and you could peel it off with your fingernails which I used to quite enjoy doing.

(Britt)

Ye canny eat yer porridge wi a fork

SLURP SLURP

Ye canny eat yer porridge wi a fork

SLURP SLURP

Ye canny eat yer porridge

Ye canny eat yer porridge

Ye canny eat yer porridge wi a fork

SLURP SLURP.

"We usually start each school talk by asking the children how many of them have tried porridge, how many like it, and how many had it for breakfast that morning, and it's great to see that this most traditional of Scottish foods is widely enjoyed by primary school children."

(from the Hamlyns Oats website)

My partner is a personal trainer and we have porridge almost every morning with almond milk and berries or other fresh fruit. I didn't like it when I was little - what child does?

(Sophie)

I love eating porridge. And I
love reading books about
"Porridge the Cat".

(Anouk, aged 6)

I make porridge for my granddaughter, Iona when she stays with me and she loves it - and not just for breakfast. If she's coming to me after school and wants a snack, she sometimes asks for porridge then as well.

(Rosella)

I like normal porridge.
I don't like the kind
with syrup in it.

(Alastair, 9)

"Can I have some more porridge, please?"

(Anna Marlene, 9, the author's granddaughter)

"Please, Sir, I want some more."

(Oliver Twist, asking for seconds of oatmeal gruel served in the workhouse, in the novel by Charles Dickens, published in 1837)

For the first time in more than 100 years, the "Manual of Workhouse Cookery" is being republished next month. It includes a recipe for gruel – a watery porridge consisting of oatmeal, treacle, water and salt.

(from a news report, 2008)

I didn't have porridge when I was a child - it was Cocoa Pops for me. But my husband and I have porridge most mornings, with chocolate protein stirred into it.

(Susan)

My husband used to make porridge for the kids when they were wee and at Christmas time, if there were any of those chocolate coins in the house, he'd put a chocolate coin in their porridge - foil taken off, obviously! - and stir it in to make chocolate porridge. *My mum made us porridge. We had it with caster sugar which was kept in one of those fancy, old-fashioned sugar shakers that people used to give as wedding presents.*

(Kirstie)

"I like porridge with fruit and/ or honey but idk how people manage to eat it with Nutella/ chocolate flavouring, it actually looks like squirrel diorrhea"

(from a student message board)

"VisitScotland, working together with Scotland Food & Drink, has today launched The Porridge Grand Tour of Scotland: a range of unique porridge-themed adventure recommendations where oat enthusiasts can indulge their love of porridge and even enjoy porridge for breakfast, lunch and dinner whilst admiring the view of rolling hills, lochs or castles."

(from a news report, 2017)

I sometimes eat porridge oats as often as three times a day – but not cooked. I have them with some milk and a bit of sugar which is the way we usually eat them in Denmark where I was brought up. It saves washing up a pot and means even young children can help themselves to a cheap, healthy snack.

(Ann Marie)

When I lived in a commune down in England, we bought porridge oats in a 25 kilo sack from the wholesaler because porridge is filling, cheap and good for you, and easy to make. It was what we had throughout the day if we were feeling hungry. You'd come in, put some rolled oats into a bowl, pour boiling water onto them and stir it around for a couple of minutes, then eat it with sugar or honey. You did have to be careful to stir all the lumps out. It also saved washing up a pot doing it that way.

(James)

The author tried this and found it not entirely satisfactory, due to lumps forming and the mixture remaining thin.

I have porridge all the time, and not just for breakfast. I was brought up on it. If I didn't have family to cook for, I'd live on porridge – and soup. Sugar? No – I didn't know anyone ate sugar with their porridge until I left home.

(Maureen)

During the 17th century, Scottish university students lived in very basic accommodation. Their diet was meagre too, largely consisting of oatmeal, which they would make into porridge. This lifestyle would remain typical until the late 19th century. Rev. James Sharp noted that as a student at the University of Edinburgh, "the liberal arts, sciences and theology were cultivated on oatmeal, with an occasional glass of beer on a Saturday night."

(wikipedia)

When I was a wee girl, I used to spend part of the summer holidays with my aunt who was matron at a hospital in Chryston. This was the 1960s when not everyone had a fridge, and my aunt really did have a porridge drawer in her kitchen table. It was lined with grease proof paper and she'd make porridge once a week, using oatmeal and a spurtle, and pour it into the drawer to let it set. Then every morning she'd cut a slice off and warm it through in a pot on the cooker. To eat it, she'd fill a tea cup with milk and dip each spoonful of porridge into the cup - no sugar - although I had sugar with mine. *It made sense doing that because she was very busy and it saved her having to cook up fresh porridge every morning.*

(Carol)

When we were living on Harris, I'd make porridge for myself and to save time in the morning, because I went out to work, I'd make a big jug of it in the microwave, divide it into four bowls, have one of them and then cover the other three with cling film and put those in the fridge. For the next three mornings, I'd take a bowl out of the fridge and heat it up in the microwave. I ate it with golden syrup and milk.

(Susan)

I can't remember what we had for breakfast when I was a child because my mum was in and out of hospital with TB so it was quite a confusing time. But after I married, we'd go up to visit my husband's parents and his father would sit by the fire with a pot on his lap, and his mother would measure porridge oats into it, then boiling water, and he'd stir it around for ages, until it reached a certain consistency. Then he'd put the pot, with the porridge in it, into a cupboard and the next day, he'd spoon some of the porridge from the pot into a bowl and pour hot milk over it. That's how he ate his porridge.

(Norma)

We never got the chance to have porridge in our house, even if we'd wanted it. Only my father was allowed to have porridge which my mother made every morning, just for him. The rest of us had cornflakes.

(Eunice)

Oats are Scotland's best export with 55 per cent of oats produced for Europe, the Middle East and Africa. Muslims use porridge to stop hunger pangs between fasting during the festival of Ramadan. A bowl of porridge will keep you full for four hours and 21 minutes and prevents between-meal snacking.

(The Sun, 2010)

One of the King's soldiers was arguing with a dusty-looking couple who had stepped down from a poor wagon covered with sacks.

"We heard they were crying out for all the produce as they can get for the King's visit!" the man said in the accent of a Scotsman.

"No Scots in the city of York while the King's here, no vagabonds," the guard said implacably.

"But we've driven from Jedburgh. We've the year's oat harvest here."

"Then serve it to thy border reivers that steal our cattle. Turn around and be off. No Scots!"

(from "Sovereign", a Tudor mystery
novel by C.J. Sansom)

The best thing about leaving home and moving into a bedsit was being able to have cornflakes for breakfast instead of porridge.

(Anna)

I wasn't brought up on porridge but as soon as I left home and got a place of my own, I started making it.

(Iain)

My mother used to say "Eat your porridge or you'll never get strong". Now I find myself saying something similar. I said to a friend the other day, when we were trying to shift something and were finding it difficult: "We need to eat porridge to give us strength".

(Viv)

My gran used to give me porridge and try to make me eat it by saying: "Do you not want to be strong like your papa?"

(Alastair)

Ma wee ma used to say
porridge stuck to your ribs
and made you bigger.

(John)

We didn't have porridge when I was growing up. But I did try it, once, when my mum was on a diet last year and she ate it every morning for months. I didn't like it. But it worked for her. She lost almost four-and-a-half stone.

(Gail)

My mum made porridge - Scott's Porage Oats. And when she was on a diet, it was porridge and grapefruit every morning. She cooked it with a bit of salt and I added more salt to mine after it was cooked, and stirred it in. No sugar for either of us. Sometimes I had Weetabix or Frosties. My dad never had porridge. He was an egg and sausage man, every day of the week.

(Gavin)

When my kids were little I began a tradition in the house that we'd start having porridge when the clocks went back, then we'd go back onto breakfast cereal when the clocks went forward. We had porridge when I was wee but never with sugar - oh god no! The first time I heard of sugar on porridge I literally couldn't believe it. I was like: "Are you crazy?!" I like it thin, almost like gruel, with a little bit of salt sprinkled on top. My kids didn't eat it when they were older but now they're giving it to their kids.

(Ginny)

I was brought up in Wales and my mum made porridge for us, although not everyday. But I never made it for my kids. It must have skipped a generation because my daughter and her boyfriend have recently moved in with me and she makes porridge for the three of us. I have mine with milk, with salt sprinkled on the top.

(Kay)

The important role of porridge in history was recently highlighted by Scots academic Alistair Moffat, who claimed the invention of porridge changed the world. He suggested that feeding youngsters porridge allowed mothers to stop breastfeeding earlier, freeing them to bear more children, in turn increasing the world's population.

(from a news report, 2012)

There were 11 children in our family. I was one of the youngest and I was very close to my mother who used to let me stand on a stool beside the cooker and stir the breakfast porridge with a spurtle. The thing was, I hated porridge so much I could hardly look at it, never mind eat it. So I had toast instead. I don't think my father would have been pleased if he had known but there were so many of us that we had to eat in shifts and he had aleady left for work by the time I had my breakfast.

(Cathie)

I've never been able to eat porridge. It's because of the way it looks - like wallpaper paste. Ugh.

(Renee)

The only porridge I can remember having as a child was when I was eight and went into hospital to have my tonsils out. It was disgusting: grey, salty, sticky stuff. How did they get it that colour?

(John)

My wife makes delicious porridge. She uses sprouted oats - because they're better for you - which need to be soaked overnight. Then she starts cooking it in water and adds home-made almond milk half way through. It makes the porridge so creamy, you'd think there was actual cream in it. Some people add sliced banana to their porridge for extra carbs and sweetness, but we don't.

(Bilal)

My dad used to make porridge on a Sunday when I was a child but these days, we make our porridge in the microwave, using sachets, and my mum stirs a handful of frozen blueberries into hers which softens the blueberries and cools the porridge down at the same time.

(Louise)

Determined to start eating (and liking) porridge more this year. First plate worked ... with nectarine, dried mulberries, toasted walnuts and maple syrup. For you mingin' traditionalists, John had his with salt and nae fruit, bleuch!! (Hazel)

Best meal oa the day - I hae mine wi blueberries, prunes, walnuts, Greek yoghurt and a wee dab oa salt - scrumptious. (Tony)

I bake 40 grammes of oats with an egg mixed through and a yogurt and some salted caramel syrup oven for 25 mins the bloody bomb. (Lesley)

I have mine with salt, chilli flakes and a poached egg on top. (Mike)

(part of the Facebook conversation that sparked the idea for this book)

I'm very old school where porridge is concerned. My wife has it with honey and fresh fruit but my idea of "exotic" where porridge is concerned is to have cream with it instead of milk, no sugar.

(Tom)

When I started working for Glasgow Museums almost 30 years ago, I was based at Pollok House and whoever got in first in the morning would put on a pot of porridge for the rest of us coming in because we started at 8.30 on cleaning the place; giving it a daily "heavy dusting" as it was called. The place was kept immaculate. It was just men on the team, mostly all coming up for retirement age, and I was known as "the boy" because I was so much younger. *I still have porridge every morning, because it's good for you. I use sachets, made in a bowl in the microwave; no salt or sugar, just milk.*

(Iain)

When I was living in London, I started work at 8.30 in the morning so I made my porridge before I went out, put it in a Tupperware box and ate it on the train on my way into work because the journey took about 30 minutes. A lot of other people on the train were eating their breakfast so it didn't look weird.

(Ruby)

My dad used to sometimes have a bowl of porridge in the evening if he was going out to meet friends at the pub. He wasn't much of a drinker and he said the porridge helped absorb the alcohol so he wouldn't get drunk.

(Jess)

I always put a layer of made up porridge between 2 pairs of socks when I'm wearing wellies, otherwise your feet freeze. It's warmer if you add salt - but not sugar. For some reason, your feet don't get wet, just nice and warm.

(from Sue's Blether Board on the internet)

Dr. Cameron: *"Janet, rejoice with me. Finlay is back to us - and see ye keep the porridge hot on the stove."*

(From "Dr. Finlay's Casebook" by A.J. Cronin)

As a child, you accept what you're given. I was given porridge for breakfast, although I think I remember Grape Nuts and another breakfast cereal. I was also given Jesus. But as an adult, you choose - and I chose porridge: oats and water in the microwave for two or three minutes, then add a few grapes and slices of orange, cut up, for your daily fresh fruit. And I also chose Jesus. *Porridge is the only way, and Jesus is THE only way!*

(man in Sauchiehall Street, giving out religious tracts)

About Deedee Cuddihy

Deedee Cuddihy is a journalist who was born and brought up in New York but has lived in Glasgow since the "Big Storm" of 1967 (which she slept through). Or was it 1968? After finishing art school in Glasgow, she realised being an artist would be too difficult - and being an art teacher would be even more difficult. So she became a journalist and has been one ever since. She is married to a Scotsman and has two grown up children - plus three granddaughters. "The Wee Guide to Porridge" is the 13th in her Funny Scottish Books series, the other titles including the best-selling "How to Murder a Haggis", "I Love Irn-Bru", "The Wee Guide to Scottish Women" and "Only in Dundee". She eats her porridge with quite a lot of brown sugar.